DISCARD

SOURCES

DEVIN JOHNSTON

SOURCES

TURTLE POINT PRESS

NEW YORK 2008

002000294567

To live is to die, to be awake is to sleep,
to be young is to be old, for the one flows
into the other, and the process is capable
of being reversed. —HERAKLEITOS

SOURCES

SLEEPING IN

Wake and sleep,
sleep and wake.

Sheets smell
of sour milk

tangled up with
pine perfume.

Outside a warbler
hurries through

its auctioneering,
each repeat

hammered by
an angry note.

Every creature
only seeks

reprieve from habit,
lives and breathes

on borrowed money,
borrowed song,

striking matches
against the sun.

CLOUDS

What and *what* and *what* and *what*
reiterate the clouds, igneous
in source and crushing weight
ten thousand feet above the earth.

Locked and forgotten in states of want,
from the kitchen sink we watch them roll
against the sun—diurnal, tidal:

spume of Puget Sound, eggs
boiled at Little Bighorn, evaporated
birdbaths on display, sunbathers
stretched beside the pool; August clouds
retentive of
                    a flashing glimpse.

We say, *that's life, that's love*—

3

Yet the active file distinguishes
hounds, greyhounds, mongrels, spaniels, curs;
gate and mirror; heads of lettuce
glazed with rain; Taj Mahal
and traveler; marching trees of
Birnam Wood; sheep from Deuteronomy.

Above the kitchen sink, we skim
a massive novel shorn of names, wild
ramifications of dis-

    appointment, old life
convoluted past recall.

HOG ISLAND OYSTERS

Oysters adhere
to things, no eyes:

spat on the smooth
curve of a pier

they feel shadows
and snap shut.

The sun wavers
while anchored below

each distills
Tomales Bay,

accreting waves
within its shell.

Voluptuous and cold,
Kumamoto trembles

on a thin fork,
liquefaction

of cloud. Rain
distorts glass,

our tavern submerged
all afternoon.

PRESERVED

Cresting the caps
on a tuna can,
a soft-chinned
western rig
trails a thousand
hooks across
fair-weather grounds.

Two pointers
on a tin of peaches
circle, sniff the air,
and freeze in the rushes
of a sopping field.

Repetition pears
cuddle in their leaves
while Time O'Day

depicts two clocks
and a bowl of beans.

Seasons, oceans,
continents
tumble from the shelves.

THE DOOR

What was this basement door
scratched by the dog,
cut from the hardest
shagbark stock?

In its shade, canebrake
stacked up, stock-
still in a shower
of rachis and bark.
Ticks crowded
summer leaves,
triggered to jump
by heat. High up,
jagged branches
made exploded
diagrams of cloud.

The straightest went
for ax hafts
turned on a lathe,
the trunk for sash
and door. From Osage,
a freight hauler
drove through smoking
rain as planks
rattled over ruts.

I know none of this,
only the dark
plumes of grain,
deep scores, and smooth
action of its lock.

SUN AND SHADOW

Fire fuses
sand to glass

and glass cracks
underfoot.

Catalpa
canopies drop

popcorn on
a Triumph's hood.

Sol y sombra!
Heat-sick

dogs froth
and paper curls.

Insulating
white sleep

I pull the shade
and stay indoors.

RELUCTANT TRAVELERS

I

One could fall asleep and float
a hundred miles off course,
or rob a restaurant in broad daylight,
or weep openly on the air.

Contretemps could snap the line
that anchors date in memory,
uproot the smell of eucalypts,
or debauch a shadow from its leaf.

Mockingbirds from Texas range
no farther north than this
chill suburb in which we sit
talking of where to go in spring.

2

Fear derives its force
from love: its own effect,
love radiates

from where I am
to where I'm not.

It amplifies, a hooded wave
racing through the dark.

3

On bare walls
the daylight rings
changes of
intensity;

everything
is on its way
to somewhere else
but walls.

Across an inland
sea of grass,
nothing stops
the sun

but cinder block
and cottonwood.
I wonder where
you've been.

LOOKING OUT

A person looking out
of a window waits for something
that never comes, but wants
a flash from the outside world.

Through upper reaches of
an elm, a face peering down
for no good reason looks
absurd above the sill, as if
a thumb stuck in its mouth.

A face at the window wears
no expression, blotted white
by darkness in the room.

SONOGRAM

Sleek as fox fur

your message nudges through
a lattice of electrons,

Nemesis through Oort clouds

or luminous fern through fog,
evergreens lost at the edge:

imaginary gains.

SUNFLOWERS IN NOVEMBER

Sunflowers in November
stoop over their own shadows,
stems hooked like bristles
on a card for Cheviot wool.

As pump-jacks nod in the distance,
reservoirs nearly empty,
heavy heads of sunflowers
dream of the rising sun.

Though we may talk of faces,
Helios is the only source
to which this face refers:
a source it can't survive.

THE PIPE

All winter afternoon
I hunted for a lost draft
of "Kaw, Vermillion, Cottonwood":
released, it might have drifted back
to Kansas. Along what was
the Oregon Trail, snow filled
a hoof print, revealing
stripes of furrows
and temporary boundaries.

Sorting through accordion files
of recipes, cream bond incised
by a Selectric, letters
of acceptance, pale blue
aerograms from England—
the detritus of a life
bound for special collections—
I found a rosewood pipe,

its charred bowl and thatched screen
resinous of 4566
Eighteenth Street. Inhaling,
I forgot my task, transported
to your sealed past:

                    inconclusive strands
of fog cascade from Twin Peaks
and break apart. A rosy-fingered
block of frozen squid, bought
at Safeway, thaws in the sink.
It smells sweet. Whistling a tune
from Harry Partch, you peel off
the speckled skin, then pull
a white feather from
each tiny parachute.

Alone, you light the pipe—
not thinking of expected guests
or cloud-chamber music, but of

Kaw, Vermillion, Cottonwood,
and hoof prints filled with snow.

DEPARTURES

As wild hogs, fresh from a wallow,
    scrape against the trunk
of a telephone pole while rushing past,
    smearing their flanks
with creosote and leaving behind
stiff bristles and splattered mud;

or a cardinal intently crushes
    carpenter ants in her bill,
then rubs their formic acid along
    her coverts and tail,
staining that dim blush
with a streak of gloss:

you kiss hard, sure to find
some happiness to savor on the plane.

CUSTOMS

At the sink, a business traveler
memorizes one hand with the other.

THE DIFFERENCE

I wake up missing what
I would no longer want.

CHESTER SLEEPING

All day you sleep on a green expanse
of couch, waking only to pursue
a trapezoid of sunlight as it glides
toward dusk. A speckled forepaw waves
and your third eyelid flicks across
a clear surface. Swallowed barks well up
as from a cave of sea lions, announcing
shadow dogs—distant, but no more
phantasmagoric than the waking world
of scent you trail from step to curb.

Here is an old trace, redolent of
vinegar and lilac, you approach
with care and apprehension. It is a dream
of what has gamboled past, archaic
filaments and plumes of sense
for which there are no human names.
Pausing, you sniff, then touch the tip
of your pink tongue to a blade of grass.

MOCKINGBIRD

We live each other's death
and die each other's life,
borrowing a cold flame
from sycamore in early leaf.
This morning, after heavy rain

the street erupts with birds:
grackles sharpen swords
and cedar waxwings strip
the vines, declaring love and war.
With tail cocked, I guard the stoop

from strangers, ill at ease.
As sunlight strikes a wheel,
I think as Sulla thought—
hostis, host and enemy
to every sound that swells my throat.

CROWS

Their caw is not
for us, but calls
to corvid, canid,
ringing out
tomorrow's *cras*
and love the dead.

Black lees
against the snow,
a murder crowns
what's left of day.
Riled by shadows
cast in bronze,

they raven trash
and mob the sun,

their wings and bills
compacted as
initials from
the Book of Kells.

TRACING

When you were young,
what buzz of ex-
pectation promised
nothing known—

what thought perplexed
as, belly down,
intensive con-
centration traced

Pegasus
from *Wonder Book*,
your pencil finding
wings and hooves

as fish rise
from cloudy beds.
When paper slips
the scale is wrong,

distorting all:
when you are young
without words
you hum the tune.

THE GOLDEN HINDE

On Christmas Day, Kathleen and I
propel a raft with plastic spoons
through the hissing fur of surf,
    stirring as we go
    an Alka-Seltzer sun.

We pass Bolinas–Stinson School,
the fire house, and Smiley's dive;
extinguished geodesic domes
    along the mesa road
    where Cream Saroyan lives.

With a telescope, my sister spies
the erstwhile chemist of Argonne
who left his post to polish glass.
    As penance, he engraves
    a glyph of hydrogen

on the blank face of every cliff
from Monterey to Inverness.
Beside us, cormorants describe
    the chop in grunts, then plunge
    through thirty feet of grease.

I try to hold my breath as long
and cheat or fail. As evening comes
we pass the final spit of land.
    Once more around the Horn
    and then we'll make for home.

BIOGRAPHY

Those who fix their minds
on what we face
in childhood—

an open door through which
the dog escapes—
carve stone, compose

romans à clef
of fine proportion,
and love without remorse.

While those who turn in sleep
to teenage years—
a labyrinth

of gaudy streets,
form turned on itself—
cannot find their fates.

Absorbed by clouds
they wander past
the Palace of the Moon,

consoled by smells
of mu xu rou,
then home to empty rooms.

FRIENDS

In the old days, when you dropped by
the bungalow on Wood Street—
your rap on the door would interrupt
my convoluted train of thought
from Fabergé to forgeries—
we argued long into the night
and wrecked the morning. You soaked up
everything in the house, nothing
was enough. Now you phone
conscientiously from an airport, busy
with a brief on failure analysis.
It seems a rail in Thunder Bay
cracked last winter, overturning
a dozen tankers; from their split sides,
methanol poured across
a frozen creek. The rail steel had proved
impure, manufactured
in the last diminished blaze
of Bethlehem, before the mills shut down.

ROMAN CANDLES

Thoughts these days, fixed on hate,
catch fire from such varied sparks
that while one quietly explodes,
a powder-blue hydrangea mop,
another shouts, *Look out below!*
One repulses, one draws near;
a crowd collects as couples dance.
Distressed, a girl tears loose her sleeve
and hisses, *Keep away from me*.

Love's not always good, and hate
cleans the soul: free of guilt,
a roman candle drowns the stars
and purges night of resonance
(*in Rome there is no room for Rome*,
a disappointed traveler wrote).
Against love, you fix your thoughts
on flame, our disposition's flag.

AFTER SAPPHO

Some say flashing metal, some say fire,
others call a Sea Harrier
in vertical ascent
                    the loveliest sight
that dark earth offers. I say
whatever you love most.

Everybody knows—every day
some Helen leaves her husband, home,
and daughter, to board a train that's bound
for Shreveport or Cheyenne

—led astray, I almost said

but that she steps
so lightly down.
Which brings to mind Elena—
she's not here.

I'd rather catch her eye
across the shop
                    counter than watch
a full squadron rise
by vectored thrust
above the dunes.

THUNDERHEADS

Days spent in the shelter of work
blow apart at dusk:

skirts rustle mimic rain
as shadows bloom across the draw;
a five-ton hammer taps
a crimped leaf; cutterheads
dredge voices through the wall.

Over Chattanooga
some latent thought unfolds:

heaped clouds detonate
a cauliflower dome,
topographies of doubt,
redoubt, lit by leaders
cloud to ground.

As the first thick drop
clings to thorn, a core
of purple cabbage stirs
Bonny James Campbell
from Cumberland Gap,
pelting river pearls.

RADIO TELEMETRY

Under rain

your whip antenna with
a solar cell

rotates, listening for
something winter

meant to say:
far north

desperate joy
without remorse

wakes and tilts
across the swale;

a slow wave
pours away.

Sifting bleeps
and bearing lines

sniff the air.
What pertains?

SWIFT-FOOTED

Look at the sun
beating down
on what was
February's cold
mud:
        everything
durable proves
unendurable.

Stage thunder
rolls from an empty
pool of galvanized
metal; sparrows
bathe in dust.

Time wounds
all heels.

AN EMBLEM OF BYZANTIUM

Fat Tail, Raven, Spark Vark.
Blackbird with your fuselage
cradled by the stars.

Raptor wreathed in flame.
Eagle wrapped in gasoline
that whistles in the dark.

Harrier and Hawk.
Hammers never took your form
from any living thing.

NAMES OF BIRDS

Von der Decken sailed *The Welf*
up the Jubba River.
Mushroom-soft with dry rot,
it foundered on the rapids.

Von der Decken's hornbill.

In the headwaters of Limpopo
stippled by a light rain,
Wahlberg waded past a herd
of elephants. A bull charged;
its tusk gored him in the chest.

Wahlberg's honeyguide and eagle.

Over Peru on Christmas Eve,
Koepcke slept through heavy rain.
Lightning struck her lost Electra,
setting its wings aflame.

Maria Koepcke's screech owl.

Speke stumbled over a stile,
discharging a shotgun at his head:
With drumming wings, a common quail
exploded from the underbrush.

STARLINGS

Starlings plunge through cold fog;
a pitchy *xerox* chafes the dawn chorus.

LOCUSTS AND WILD HONEY

Even the dog cocks his ear
when called. Magnetic name:

in a wilderness of sense I clear
a space for pride and shame.

THE GHOSTWRITER

Years ago, between the drift
of Harvard and another life,
I met the great philanthropist
von Hempel: as I held the door
ajar, he quoted Edmund Burke
on manners as the root of all
our rights (his were impeccable).
That night, as I sat pouring through
employment ads, he telephoned
and in some telepathic flash
abruptly hired me to ghost
a family history—"for those
von Hempels scattered and remote."

I set to work each afternoon
in an airless office high above
the stock exchange, transcribing tapes

of interviews: "a dragonfly
across the plains—was that the time
we stole a cake—was that the time—"

From the lacquered desk at which I sat
a violent hieroglyph by Kline
exploded from von Hempel's head.

Foundries in Berlin, disease,
hardscrabble lives, the crossing, all
those years were but a preface to
my central theme—the wealth amassed
through steaming gin distilleries
    in central Illinois:
    a heartless elder son,
    a younger son ill-used;
the hammer coming down, and laws
of Prussian primogeniture.

When the work was done, I felt it mine
so tangled with it were my thoughts.
Von Hempel chose a title—*Time
Distilled*—and gave the manuscript

to Imogene, his only child.
"I wept to read the passage on
  your uncle, Otto's younger son—
    the eclipse in which he lived and died."
  She sadly smiled and took his hand.
"I wept in writing it," he said.

CIRCUMSPECT

Those I wait on
wait for me
to halve a lemon
with one chop,
wedge a spoon
between the rind
and pulp, rotate,
then drop its core
down the drain.

At table eight,
beehive sips
Campari with
a sour face;
at table three,
canary blazer
breaks a glass,

then laughs as if
he owned the place.

Circumspect,
I weave between
chairs pushed back,
waiting for
the shift's end
and morning to unwind.

Brushing past,
I lightly spin
the order wheel,
no wonder
of obligation but
an empty
hoop of metal.

PACKING UP

An Irish tea table
someone took as spoils

no longer speaks,
inured to use.

Having crawled beneath
to disconnect the phone,

I constellate
wormholes in deal,

black stars
to guide us through

whatever things
we fought about,

hooded forms
of rage and grief.

From slipper foot
to C-scroll,

traffic of a dead world
is testing a technique

by which to make
intentions clear:

you walk,
and on the tabletop

a glass of water
trembles.

REVENANTS

Cessation of pulse
and breath

means gone without
moving

or come, an end
to coming and going.

What's left
feeds off

memory, bloodless
but strong.

Sometimes caught
out at dawn,

a revenant
gets talked about

across the kitchen
counter,

you and not
nether and neither

very old
and new.

AFTER PROPERTIUS

Ghosts do exist: death is not entire.
A cloud of smoke escapes the funeral pyre.
Though lately buried beside the road,
Cynthia seemed to lean above my bed
when after jerking off—half in a dream—

I found my sheets a chill and lonely realm.
She had the selfsame hair, the selfsame eyes;
her shroud was burned into her side.
The flames had gnawed her favorite silver band
and the river Lethe had chafed her lips with sand.
Her breath was warm, but as she spoke I heard
her brittle fingers rattle like a gourd.

"Traitor—from whom I should expect as much—
can sleep already have you in its clutch?
Have secrets of Pigalle, where evenings end

57

at four A.M., already slipped your mind?
For you, how many times I shinnied down
a gutter pipe or trellis to the ground,
embracing on the sidewalk where we met,
hugging beneath our coats to find some heat.
Think of the secret oaths, each word a lie,
the wind has torn apart so heedlessly!

"As I fell from sight and mind, no one spoke
a sympathetic word, no watchman shook
a castanet to keep my spirit safe,
no pillow couched my head above the earth.
In short, who saw you stoop beside my bier,
your borrowed gabardine grown damp with tears?
If 'March was a busy time,' you might at least
have stepped into the road to see me pass.
Had you no thought to mingle with my smoke
a pinch of sandalwood—to bring me luck?
Did you never think to gather irises,
or spill a drop of wine and break the glass?

"Burn René for poisoning my mind
with acid gossip as I sipped his wine

and Nikki for perverted appetites
kept hidden: brand them both with cigarettes.
Once Mina sold herself, and now she signs
the dust with a hem of gold, and if she finds
some waitress rhapsodizing on my grace
she huffs and puffs to have the girl replaced.
Because a niece brought lilacs for my tomb
or sister asked a favor in my name,
Mina bound the one to a rocking chair
and whipped the other, hung by her twisted hair.
While you stood by, she melted down my gold
relief—a dowry from my dying coals.

"But I won't hound you for these bitter wrongs,
  Propertius: in your books my reign was long.
  I swear by rhymes that cannot be reversed
  and engine-idle growls of Cerberus
  I never strayed—and if I lie, may boas
  writhe in hissing knots above my bones.

"Few living know the river Lethe divides,
  distributaries branching left and right.
  One channel carries Clytemnestra's taint

59

and the monstrous, artificial cow of Crete
through which a woman mated with a bull,
its plastic carapace a rocking hull.
On the other branch, a riverboat descends
with flags unfurled in honeysuckle winds.
An orchestra assembles on the deck
with cymbals, double bass, and clarinet.
Andromeda and Hypermestra, wives
remembered in the stars, speak of their lives:
the first reveals her forearms, badly bruised
from frozen chains, an undeserved abuse;
the second tells of how her sisters dared
to stab their bridegrooms—only hers was spared.
And so our loves are ratified by tears,
our lives by death. I hid your faults for years.

"If any feeling penetrates the fog
of pot that you and Mina smoke, I beg,
support my mom, and keep my looking glass
untouched by any other woman's glance.
Burn the books you seeded with my name
and stop amassing poems by my fame—
uproot that English ivy from my grave

before it binds my bones with twisted leaves.
Where the Seine River forms a horseshoe bend,
a dark exactitude through sunlit land,
inscribe an epitaph in native stone
that city passengers might glimpse at dawn:
Here lie golden Cynthia's remains
reflecting glory on the mighty Seine.

"A dream that comes through cemetery gates
should not be shaken off, but given weight.
Night frees the cloistered shadows and we roam;
then Cerberus himself may stray from home.
At dawn, the laws command we rendezvous
beside the river Lethe, a lifeless slough.

"For now, let others have you: I alone
will keep you, grinding bone entwined with bones."

Having closed this argument and case,
her shadow fell away from my embrace.

AVEC GLAÇON

Phases, nerves:

furred on one side
an ice cube cracks,

fasces of silver
needles at its core

2

Across the lily
pond, not optic nerves

but pewter plate
this afternoon,

Hokusai has built
a little bridge

3

Among our speculations

the last foliole
of tender leaf

makes so light a point

that even dragonflies
can only hover near,

imponderable

.

FOUR NIGHTS

JEKYLL ISLAND

Clouds. Mars.

Waves detonate
a cold piano.

WOLLONGONG

A wave, a welter
of clouds cross-
hatched with rain:

excess, happiness.

HANNIBAL

Flickering black between
consecutive stills,
rain rattles leaves.

Tin foil strips
light from the moon.

The very eye of night
nestles beneath its lid.

FIEND'S FELL

Blotting paper,
licorice,
velvet slug on slate;

clothes closet,
Horsehead,
Coalsack in Crux.

Down silent lanes
of afterlife
all rush to fill the gap.

IN THE NORTH

A blast off the Atlantic
snaps a flag in the Firth
of Clyde, while thirty leagues
away, the same synoptic wind
surges across this hillside
honeycombed with mineshafts,
sounding the unstopped slots
of a "G" harmonica left
to dry on the kitchen sill.
Snow charges a sky
in which the sun swims
and glimmers like a groat,
a turbulent space where owls
hunt by day but nothing
stands for long—bereft
of circumstance—beyond
the standing stones of
Long Meg and Her Daughters.

Through the night, like a stoker
on a fast express—the Hyperion
on its Edinburgh run—
you hoy buckets of coal
on the grate, only to see
its flames drawn up
the chimney, getting more
heat from hoying the fuel
than from its burning.
As a barnacle goose swims
against the dark, uttering
its terse honk, you pull
your favorite word, *duvet*,
close about your head.
Tomorrow, bailiffs may
take everything
not hammered down.

RETURNING

Returning from
      a night of close,
            protracted talk

to bed, we love
      blankness most,
            not sleep

but possibility.
      It waits, stiff
            and innocent

as Lorca's
      farther than
        the seas.

Blue pierced
      white, sheets
            billow above

the fixity
      of box springs,
            air tints

sunshine and snow.
      Turning, you frap
            the covers: keel

drags low,
      slicing through
            cold brine.

Though separately,
      we raise
            an island from

the open sea
      with flashing
            thoughts for sails.

THE GREEKS

Ladder and source,
we find no ease

never quite
at home at home.

No, never, not
darken the page

in a childish script.
Winter has come.

Ladders lean
against the sky,

sources whistle
past our lips.

Pacing rugs
or battered roads

we wait for what
we know we know.

ACKNOWLEDGMENTS

My epigraph comes from *Seven Greeks: Translations* by Guy Davenport (New Directions, 1995), 170.

Versions of these poems have appeared in the following publications: *Boxkite, Bridge, The Canary, Chicago Review, Cordite Poetry Review, The Cultural Society, Damn the Caesars, Fascicle, GutCult, LVNG, Near South, New American Writing, Poetry, Public Space, Salt, Shearsman, Slope, Threepenny Review, Twenty-Six, Xantippe,* and *Zoland Poetry.*

Some of these poems also appeared in the following chapbooks: *Looking Out* (LVNG Supplemental Series, 2004), a collaboration with the artist Brian Calvin; and *Sources* (Empty Hands Broadside, 2007).

ABOUT THE AUTHOR

Born in 1970, Devin Johnston is the author of two previous books of poetry, *Aversions* (Omnidawn, 2004) and *Telepathy* (Paper Bark Press, 2001). His book of criticism, *Precipitations: Contemporary American Poetry as Occult Practice*, appeared from Wesleyan University Press in 2002. He co-directs Flood Editions, an independent publishing house, and teaches at Saint Louis University.